Personal Growth and Productivity: Best Practices for Success

Nova Starling

Copyright © 2024 Nova Starling

All rights reserved.

ISBN: 9798332966842

DEDICATION

This book is dedicated to all the individuals striving to better themselves and reach their fullest potential. It is for those who wake up each day with a desire to grow, learn, and achieve. Your journey towards personal growth and productivity is a testament to your dedication, perseverance, and resilience.

To the Dreamers and Doers:

May this guide serve as a beacon of inspiration and a source of practical strategies, providing you with the best practices to navigate the complexities of life.

To the Lifelong Learners:

Your commitment to continuous improvement and your insatiable curiosity drive progress and innovation. May you find in these pages the tools and insights needed to sustain your journey of learning and development.

To the Goal-Setters and Achievers:

Your determination to set and reach ambitious goals is commendable. This book is a testament to your efforts and aims to support you with best practices that will enhance your productivity and personal growth.

To My Family and Friends:

Your unwavering support and encouragement have been my anchor. This work is as much a reflection of your love and belief in me as it is a guide for others.

To Every Reader:

Thank you for choosing this book. I hope it provides you with valuable insights and practical strategies to help you achieve your goals and realize your potential. May the best practices shared in these pages inspire and guide you towards a fulfilling and productive life.

CONTENTS

1. Introduction
2. Understanding Personal Growth
   - The Importance of Personal Growth
   - How to Foster Personal Growth
   - Self-Reflection Exercises
3. Setting Effective Goals
   - The SMART Criteria
   - Creating an Action Plan
   - Staying Motivated
   - Real-Life Goal-Setting Examples
4. Developing a Growth Mindset
   - The Power of a Growth Mindset
   - Strategies for Developing a Growth Mindset
   - Overcoming Limiting Beliefs
   - Growth Mindset Case Studies
5. Time Management Techniques
   - Popular Time Management Techniques
   - Tips for Effective Time Management
   - Weekly Planning and Review
   - Time Management Case Studies
6. Building Healthy Habits
   - Understanding Habit Formation
   - Strategies for Building Healthy Habits
   - Breaking Bad Habits
   - Habit Formation Case Studies
7. Overcoming Obstacles
   - Common Obstacles and How to Overcome Them
   - Turning Setbacks into Opportunities
   - Developing Resilience
   - Personal Stories of Overcoming Obstacles
8. Enhancing Productivity
   - Techniques for Enhancing Productivity
   - Staying Organized
   - Productivity Tools and Apps
   - Real-Life Productivity Tips
9. Building Meaningful Relationships
   - Building Healthy Relationships
   - Networking and Collaboration
   - Improving Communication Skills
   - Relationship Building Exercises
10. Mindfulness and Well-being

- Mindfulness Practices
- Meditation Techniques
- Stress Management Strategies
- Mindfulness Exercises

11. Continuous Learning
    - The Importance of Lifelong Learning
    - Methods for Continuous Learning
    - Resources for Learning and Development
    - Learning Success Stories

12. Conclusion

1 Introduction

Welcome to "Master Your Life," a comprehensive guide designed to help you unlock your full potential. In this book, you'll discover practical strategies and tips to achieve personal growth, enhance productivity, and live a more fulfilling life. Whether you're looking to improve your career, relationships, or overall well-being, this book will provide you with the tools you need to succeed. Let's begin your journey to a better you.

2 Understanding Personal Growth

Personal growth is a lifelong journey of self-improvement and self-discovery. It's about setting goals, challenging yourself, and continuously striving to become the best version of yourself. In this chapter, we'll explore the concept of personal growth, its importance, and how it can transform your life.

The Importance of Personal Growth

Personal growth is essential for leading a fulfilling and meaningful life. It involves expanding your knowledge, developing new skills, and improving your mental and emotional well-being. By continuously working on personal growth, you can achieve greater success, happiness, and satisfaction in all areas of your life.

How to Foster Personal Growth

1. **Self-Reflection:** Regularly take time to reflect on your thoughts, actions, and experiences. This helps you gain insights into your strengths, weaknesses, and areas for improvement.
2. **Goal Setting:** Set clear, achievable goals that align with your values and aspirations. This gives you direction and motivation to keep moving forward.
3. **Continuous Learning:** Stay curious and open to new experiences. Seek out opportunities to learn and grow, whether through formal education, reading, or life experiences.
4. **Adaptability:** Be open to change and willing to adapt to new circumstances. Embrace challenges as opportunities for growth rather than obstacles.

Self-Reflection Exercises

1. **Daily Journaling:** Spend 10-15 minutes each day writing about your thoughts, feelings, and experiences.
2. **Weekly Review:** At the end of each week, review your achievements, challenges, and areas for improvement.
3. **Monthly Goals Assessment:** Assess your progress towards your goals on a monthly basis and adjust your plans as needed.

Personal Growth Stories

- **Story of Steve Jobs:** How his passion for learning and relentless pursuit of excellence led to the creation of Apple.
- **Story of Oprah Winfrey:** Overcoming significant personal and professional obstacles to become a global icon and philanthropist.
- **Story of Malala Yousafzai:** Her journey from a young girl in Pakistan to a global advocate for girls' education.

3 Setting Effective Goals

Setting goals is crucial for personal development. Learn how to set SMART goals (Specific, Measurable, Achievable, Relevant, Time-bound) that will guide you towards success. We'll discuss techniques for defining your objectives, creating action plans, and staying motivated.

The SMART Criteria

1. **Specific:** Clearly define your goal. What exactly do you want to achieve?
2. **Measurable:** Determine how you will measure your progress and success.
3. **Achievable:** Ensure your goal is realistic and attainable given your current resources and constraints.
4. **Relevant:** Make sure your goal aligns with your broader life objectives and values.
5. **Time-bound:** Set a deadline for achieving your goal to create a sense of urgency.

Creating an Action Plan

1. **Break Down Goals:** Divide your main goal into smaller, manageable tasks.
2. **Set Milestones:** Identify key milestones to track your progress.
3. **Allocate Resources:** Determine what resources (time, money, skills) you need to achieve your goal.
4. **Schedule Tasks:** Create a timeline for completing each task.

Staying Motivated

1. **Visualize Success:** Regularly visualize the successful completion of your goal.
2. **Reward Yourself:** Celebrate small victories along the way.
3. **Stay Accountable:** Share your goals with someone who can hold you accountable.

Real-Life Goal-Setting Examples

1. **Career Advancement:** Setting and achieving a promotion goal within your company.
2. **Health and Fitness:** Creating a workout plan and tracking progress towards fitness goals.
3. **Learning and Development:** Setting a goal to learn a new skill or language within a specific timeframe.

Goal Setting Worksheets

- **SMART Goal Worksheet:** A template to help you define and plan your goals.
- **Action Plan Template:** A step-by-step guide to creating your action plan.
- **Milestone Tracker:** A tool to track your progress towards key milestones.

4 Developing a Growth Mindset

A growth mindset is the belief that abilities and intelligence can be developed through dedication and hard work. Discover how to cultivate a growth mindset, overcome limiting beliefs, and embrace challenges as opportunities for growth.

The Power of a Growth Mindset

1. **Embrace Challenges:** View challenges as opportunities to learn and grow.
2. **Learn from Criticism:** Use constructive feedback to improve your skills.
3. **Celebrate Effort:** Recognize and reward effort rather than just outcomes.
4. **Persevere Through Setbacks:** Understand that failure is a part of the learning process.

Strategies for Developing a Growth Mindset

1. **Change Your Self-Talk:** Replace negative self-talk with positive affirmations.
2. **Seek Out Learning Opportunities:** Continuously look for ways to expand your knowledge and skills.
3. **Surround Yourself with Growth-Oriented People:** Engage with others who have a growth mindset.
4. **Reflect on Your Progress:** Regularly assess your growth and set new challenges.

Overcoming Limiting Beliefs

1. **Identify Limiting Beliefs:** Recognize thoughts and beliefs that hold you back.
2. **Challenge These Beliefs:** Question the validity of your limiting beliefs and replace them with empowering ones.
3. **Take Action:** Act in ways that contradict your limiting beliefs to build new, positive habits.

Growth Mindset Case Studies

1. **Thomas Edison:** Overcoming numerous failures to invent the light bulb.
2. **J.K. Rowling:** Persisting through multiple rejections before publishing the Harry Potter series.
3. **Michael Jordan:** Embracing failures and setbacks to become one of the greatest basketball players of all time.

Exercises for Cultivating a Growth Mindset

1. **Growth Mindset Affirmations:** Daily affirmations to reinforce a growth mindset.
2. **Challenge Journal:** Document challenges you face and how you overcome them.
3. **Feedback Reflection:** Regularly seek and reflect on feedback to improve.

5 Time Management Techniques

Popular Time Management Techniques

1. **Pomodoro Technique:** Work in focused intervals (usually 25 minutes) followed by short breaks.
2. **Eisenhower Matrix:** Prioritize tasks based on their urgency and importance.
3. **Time Blocking:** Allocate specific time blocks for different activities throughout your day.
4. **Pareto Principle (80/20 Rule):** Focus on the 20% of tasks that bring 80% of the results.
5. **Getting Things Done (GTD):** Capture, process, organize, review, and engage with tasks.

Tips for Effective Time Management

1. **Plan Your Day:** Start each day with a clear plan and set priorities.
2. **Eliminate Distractions:** Identify and minimize distractions in your environment.
3. **Delegate Tasks:** Delegate or outsource tasks that others can do more efficiently.
4. **Take Breaks:** Regular breaks help maintain focus and productivity.
5. **Review and Adjust:** Regularly review your schedule and make necessary adjustments.

Weekly Planning and Review

1. **Set Weekly Goals:** Identify key objectives for the week.
2. **Schedule Tasks:** Plan your week in advance, allocating time for each task.
3. **Review Progress:** At the end of the week, review your achievements and adjust your plans as needed.

Time Management Case Studies

1. **Elon Musk:** Time blocking and extreme focus on high-impact tasks.
2. **Warren Buffett:** Prioritizing tasks based on their long-term value.
3. **Oprah Winfrey:** Balancing multiple roles and responsibilities through effective scheduling.

Time Management Worksheets

1. **Daily Planner Template:** Plan your day hour by hour.
2. **Weekly Planner Template:** Outline your week's activities.
3. **Task Priority Matrix:** Organize tasks by urgency and importance.

6 Building Healthy Habits

Habits shape our lives. Learn how to build and maintain healthy habits that support your personal growth. We'll cover habit formation, the science behind habits, and strategies for breaking bad habits.

Understanding Habit Formation

1. **The Habit Loop:** Cue, Routine, Reward.
2. **The 21/90 Rule:** It takes 21 days to build a habit and 90 days to make it a lifestyle.
3. **The Power of Consistency:** Small, consistent actions lead to significant changes.

Strategies for Building Healthy Habits

1. **Start Small:** Begin with small, manageable changes.
2. **Be Consistent:** Perform the habit at the same time each day.
3. **Use Triggers:** Link new habits to existing routines.
4. **Track Your Progress:** Use habit trackers to monitor your progress.

Breaking Bad Habits

1. **Identify Triggers:** Recognize what triggers the bad habit.
2. **Replace with Positive Habits:** Substitute the bad habit with a healthier one.
3. **Use Support Systems:** Seek support from friends, family, or support groups.
4. **Stay Patient and Persistent:** Breaking habits takes time and effort.

Habit Formation Case Studies

1. **Stephen King:** His writing routine and how it helped him publish numerous books.
2. **Serena Williams:** Daily practice and discipline leading to success in tennis.
3. **Benjamin Franklin:** His daily schedule for self-improvement.

Habit Tracker Templates

1. **Daily Habit Tracker:** Monitor daily habits.
2. **Weekly Habit Tracker:** Track habits over a week.
3. **Monthly Habit Tracker:** Review your habits monthly.

7 Overcoming Obstacles

Life is filled with challenges. Learn strategies for overcoming obstacles, turning setbacks into opportunities, and developing resilience.

Common Obstacles and How to Overcome Them

1. **Procrastination:** Techniques to overcome procrastination.
2. **Fear of Failure:** Embrace failure as a learning opportunity.
3. **Lack of Motivation:** Strategies to boost and maintain motivation.
4. **Time Constraints:** Efficiently manage time to overcome time-related challenges.

Turning Setbacks into Opportunities

1. **Reframe the Situation:** Look at setbacks from a different perspective.
2. **Learn from Mistakes:** Analyze what went wrong and learn from it.
3. **Adapt and Adjust:** Be flexible and willing to change your approach.

Developing Resilience

1. **Build a Support System:** Surround yourself with supportive people.
2. **Stay Positive:** Maintain a positive outlook even during tough times.
3. **Practice Self-Care:** Take care of your physical and mental health.

4. **Set Realistic Expectations:** Understand that progress takes time.

Personal Stories of Overcoming Obstacles

1. **Nick Vujicic:** Living a full life despite being born without limbs.
2. **Helen Keller:** Overcoming the challenges of being blind and deaf.
3. **Jim Carrey:** From homelessness to becoming a successful actor.

Resilience Building Exercises

1. **Gratitude Journaling:** Write down things you are grateful for.
2. **Mindfulness Meditation:** Practice mindfulness to stay present and calm.
3. **Physical Exercise:** Engage in regular physical activity to boost resilience.

8 Enhancing Productivity

Boost your productivity with proven techniques and tools. Learn how to stay organized, manage your time effectively, and use technology to your advantage.

Techniques for Enhancing Productivity

1. **Batch Processing:** Group similar tasks together.
2. **Deep Work:** Focus on complex tasks without distractions.
3. **Pareto Principle:** Focus on the tasks that yield the most results.
4. **Time Tracking:** Monitor how you spend your time to identify inefficiencies.

Staying Organized

1. **Declutter Your Workspace:** Keep your workspace tidy and organized.
2. **Digital Organization:** Use folders and tags to organize digital files.
3. **Task Lists:** Keep a to-do list to track tasks and priorities.
4. **Calendars and Planners:** Use calendars to plan your time effectively.

Productivity Tools and Apps

1. **Task Management Apps:** Tools like Todoist, Asana, and Trello.
2. **Time Tracking Apps:** Tools like Toggl and RescueTime.
3. **Note-Taking Apps:** Tools like Evernote and OneNote.

4. **Calendar Apps:** Tools like Google Calendar and Microsoft Outlook.

Real-Life Productivity Tips

1. **Richard Branson:** Delegation and time management.
2. **Bill Gates:** Prioritizing tasks and continuous learning.
3. **Arianna Huffington:** Importance of sleep and well-being.

Productivity Planner Templates

1. **Daily Productivity Planner:** Plan and prioritize your daily tasks.
2. **Weekly Productivity Planner:** Outline your weekly goals and tasks.
3. **Monthly Productivity Planner:** Set and track monthly objectives.

9 Building Meaningful Relationships

Healthy relationships are crucial for personal and professional success. Learn how to build and maintain meaningful relationships through effective communication and collaboration.

Building Healthy Relationships

1. **Active Listening:** Listen to understand, not just to respond.
2. **Empathy and Understanding:** Show empathy and try to understand others' perspectives.
3. **Trust and Respect:** Build trust and show respect in your interactions.
4. **Quality Time:** Spend quality time with the people who matter.

Networking and Collaboration

1. **Expand Your Network:** Attend events and join groups to meet new people.
2. **Collaborate Effectively:** Work with others to achieve common goals.
3. **Give and Receive Feedback:** Provide constructive feedback and be open to receiving it.
4. **Build Mutual Support:** Create relationships where both parties support each other.

Improving Communication Skills

1. **Clear and Concise Communication:** Be clear and to the point.

2. **Non-Verbal Communication:** Pay attention to body language and facial expressions.
3. **Conflict Resolution:** Resolve conflicts in a healthy and constructive manner.
4. **Public Speaking:** Improve your public speaking skills to communicate effectively.

Relationship Building Exercises

1. **Active Listening Exercise:** Practice active listening with a partner.
2. **Empathy Exercise:** Try to see things from another person's perspective.
3. **Trust-Building Activities:** Engage in activities that build trust.
4. **Communication Role-Play:** Practice communication skills through role-play.

Case Studies on Relationship Building

1. **Dale Carnegie:** Building relationships through effective communication.
2. **Warren Buffett and Charlie Munger:** A successful professional partnership.
3. **Oprah Winfrey and Gayle King:** Maintaining a strong personal friendship over the years.

10 Mindfulness and Well-being

Mindfulness and well-being are essential for a balanced and fulfilling life. Learn mindfulness practices, meditation techniques, and stress management strategies.

Mindfulness Practices

1. **Mindful Breathing:** Focus on your breath to stay present.
2. **Body Scan Meditation:** Scan your body to release tension.
3. **Mindful Eating:** Pay attention to the taste, texture, and smell of your food.
4. **Mindful Walking:** Be present while walking, noticing each step.

Meditation Techniques

1. **Guided Meditation:** Use guided meditations to focus your mind.
2. **Loving-Kindness Meditation:** Cultivate compassion for yourself and others.
3. **Transcendental Meditation:** Use a mantra to reach a state of deep relaxation.
4. **Zen Meditation (Zazen):** Sit in a specific posture and focus on breathing to achieve mindfulness and clarity.

Stress Management Strategies

1. **Identify Stressors:** Recognize the sources of your stress.
2. **Healthy Coping Mechanisms:** Use healthy strategies such as exercise, hobbies, and social support.

3. **Relaxation Techniques:** Practice techniques like progressive muscle relaxation and visualization.
4. **Time Management:** Manage your time effectively to reduce stress.

Mindfulness Exercises

1. **Daily Gratitude Practice:** Write down three things you are grateful for each day.
2. **Mindful Journaling:** Reflect on your thoughts and feelings through journaling.
3. **Mindfulness Breaks:** Take short breaks throughout the day to practice mindfulness.
4. **Breathing Exercises:** Use deep breathing techniques to calm your mind.

Personal Stories of Mindfulness

1. **Thich Nhat Hanh:** His teachings on mindfulness and living in the present moment.
2. **Jon Kabat-Zinn:** Development of the Mindfulness-Based Stress Reduction (MBSR) program.
3. **Eckhart Tolle:** Insights on mindfulness and presence from "The Power of Now."

11 Continuous Learning

Lifelong learning is key to personal and professional growth. Discover the importance of continuous learning, methods for acquiring new knowledge, and resources for ongoing development.

The Importance of Lifelong Learning

1. **Adapting to Change:** Stay relevant in a constantly changing world.
2. **Personal Fulfillment:** Find joy and satisfaction in learning new things.
3. **Professional Growth:** Enhance your skills and advance your career.
4. **Mental Agility:** Keep your mind sharp and engaged.

Methods for Continuous Learning

1. **Formal Education:** Pursue degrees, certifications, and courses.
2. **Self-Directed Learning:** Use books, online courses, and podcasts.
3. **Experiential Learning:** Learn through hands-on experiences and real-world challenges.
4. **Peer Learning:** Engage in study groups, mentorship, and networking.

Resources for Learning and Development

1. **Online Learning Platforms:** Websites like Coursera,

Udemy, and Khan Academy.

2. **Books and Publications:** Reading materials on various subjects.

3. **Workshops and Seminars:** Attend in-person and virtual events.

4. **Professional Organizations:** Join groups related to your field for resources and networking.

Learning Success Stories

1. **Malcolm X:** Self-education and transformation through reading.

2. **Marie Curie:** Lifelong dedication to scientific research and discovery.

3. **Elon Musk:** Learning complex subjects through intensive self-study.

Learning Plan Templates

1. **Personal Development Plan:** Outline your learning goals and strategies.

2. **Skills Tracker:** Monitor your progress in developing new skills.

3. **Learning Log:** Keep a record of what you've learned and reflections on your experiences.

12 Conclusion

Recap of Key Points

Summarize the main insights and strategies discussed throughout the book. Highlight the importance of personal growth, effective goal-setting, developing a growth mindset, managing time, building healthy habits, overcoming obstacles, enhancing productivity, building meaningful relationships, practicing mindfulness, and continuous learning.

Encouragement for the Journey Ahead

1. **Stay Committed:** Personal growth is a lifelong journey that requires dedication and perseverance.
2. **Embrace Challenges:** View challenges as opportunities to learn and grow.
3. **Celebrate Progress:** Acknowledge and celebrate your achievements, no matter how small.
4. **Seek Support:** Surround yourself with supportive people who encourage your growth.

Final Thoughts

Reflect on the transformative power of personal growth and productivity. Encourage readers to take the lessons learned and apply them to their lives, continually striving to become the best version of themselves.

www.ingramcontent.com/pod-product-compliance
Lightning Source LLC
Chambersburg PA
CBHW072058230526
45479CB00010B/1133